BIBLE LESSONS
IN THE
KITCHEN

Activities
for Children
5 & Up

ELAINE MAGEE
MPH, RD

C H R O N I M E D   P U B L I S H I N G

Bible Lessons In The Kitchen: Activities for Children 5 & Up © 1997 by Elaine Magee, MPH, RD

Library of Congress Cataloging-in-Publication Data
Magee, Elaine
Bible Lessons In The Kitchen / by Elaine Magee

      p.   cm.

Includes index.

ISBN 1-56561-124-1; $11.95

Edited by: Jolene Steffer
Cover Design: Kathy Kruger
Text Design & Production: David Enyeart
Art/Production Manager: Claire Lewis

Published by
Chronimed Publishing
P.O. Box 59032
Minneapolis, MN 55459-0032

10   9   8   7   6   5   4   3   2   1

I dedicate this book to all the people and places in my life that help keep my faith strong; all the people at St. Andrew's Presbyterian Church in Pleasant Hill, California, and all the people at Woodlands Christian Elementary in Walnut Creek, California.

ACKNOWLEDGMENTS

Special thanks to Rev. Mary McKnight and Rev. Shel White for their unfailing expertise during this loving project. And thanks to all the third graders at St. Andrew's who offered their time and taste buds to make this project come to life.

FOREWORD

Psychologists and educators have been telling us for years that some people learn visually, others learn through hearing, while others learn best by touching. Elaine Magee has found a way to teach great truths of the Bible using all three senses. In this book, she provides what she gave to the children of our church: fun, nutritious, interactive, and community-building Bible lessons. As one of the pastors of St. Andrew's Presbyterian Church, I am so pleased that Elaine brought to our congregation an exciting method for children (and adults) to discover the church as an enjoyable, tasty, nourishing place.

Elaine's first phone call to me about this subject was the beginning of my own discovery of how much the Bible has to say about food. In the New Revised Standard Version of the Bible, food is mentioned 279 times, bread 302 times, and to eat or eating 695 times!

From beginning to end, the Bible talks about food. Old Testament prophets gave the Hebrew people good news and bad news, often based on the lack or abundance of food. Jesus used food as the focus of parables and miracles. The Apostle Paul employed metaphors dealing with food to help us better understand our faith.

In the pages of this book, we will find three different approaches to Biblical learning. First, we observe Bible passages where a certain type of food is the object of what God is communicating. For example, children make bread and hear about how God provided Manna from Heaven. Second, we see how food can be used to teach concepts. The Bible was not written for children, yet even children can learn difficult concepts through interaction with common symbols. Body-shaped bread can be used to teach children about how each of us is a valuable part of the Body of Christ. Third, we see how children learn to use food for ministry. Children grasp a vital teaching of Jesus when they help make a meal for someone in need.

What could be more natural for children than getting their hands sticky with the food God has given them? God wants to feed us physically, emotionally, and spiritually. What an important concept to teach our children.

Dr. Shel White, Pastor
St. Andrew's Presbyterian Church
Pleasant Hill, California

TABLE OF CONTENTS

INTRODUCTION

I never thought I would one day be thumbing through the Holy Bible in order to write a cookbook. But after I started, merging the Bible and cooking seemed like the most natural thing in the world. Sure, I learned many Bible stories and verses as a child, but reading them again as an adult, and teaching them to children, was immensely meaningful to me.

Frankly, I don't know who had more fun —or learned more—doing these food activities, the adults or the kids. In fact, when I was working on "Ten Commandments Cake," my husband and I were hard pressed to come up with all 10 off the top of our heads. Certainly many of us adults can benefit from *Bible Lessons in the Kitchen,* too!

It all started when my church asked me to conduct cooking classes once a month for the third grade Sunday schoolers. The classes began as a way to add something a little different to the regular Sunday school schedule. But they very quickly became among the most popular church youth activities. And the Sunday school teachers have come to rely on the kitchen activities to supplement the lessons they are teaching in class.

Bible Lessons in the Kitchen is a collection of kitchen activities for children age 5 and up, that could be used in Sunday school or at home. The activities reinforce common Sunday school messages and Bible stories, such as the story of baby Moses, the Ten Commandments, the story of Easter, and the birth of Christ. Applicable scripture is also reviewed with each activity, again drawing the children toward the Bible in a new, fun way.

The children love coming to the kitchen to cook. It helps make Sunday school or time at home special. And it offers another way to reinforce Christ's teachings, the Bible, and lessons taught in Sunday school. But not just any kitchen activity will do. These activities need to be simple and quick, mainly because what little time there is needs to be split between Sunday school and the kitchen.

At my church, one group of children comes to the kitchen for the activity, then goes back to their classroom for Sunday school. The second group of children goes to Sunday school first then comes to the kitchen once the first group of cooks is finished. Children in this age group often attend the first part of church and then join together for Sunday school, leaving even less time for cooking and Sunday school.

If there is something that needs to be baked, the children return to the kitchen to collect their food treasures after Sunday school. Sometimes, the end results are even shared with the rest of the congregation during coffee hour.

The lessons in this book are general enough to incorporate all Christian denominations. All Christian faiths will be able to use this activity book because it is based on scripture from the Holy Bible.

Bible Lessons in the Kitchen can be used at Sunday schools across America or it can be used as a home-based activity to supplement church or school. It's a great way for parents to spend valuable time with their children, particularly on Sunday. It's also a new and interesting way of bringing the Bible into our everyday lives.

TIPS FOR THE TEACHERS

Each of you brings your own unique strengths and experiences to the teaching kitchen. Some of you may be very comfortable cooking but less experienced managing a group of excited children. Others may be quite familiar with the art of teaching but innocent when it comes to cracking an egg or kneading bread. Just so we all start off on almost the same foot, I've listed some tips that may help you with both the cooking and the teaching side of *Bible Lessons in the Kitchen*.

MINIMIZING CHAOS IN THE KITCHEN

1. RULES, RULES, AND MORE RULES. On the first cooking day, I would strongly suggest you lay your ground rules right on the table where the children can see them. Let them know what you will not tolerate in cooking class. Tell them what the consequences will be if the rules aren't followed. Mention that there are rules for safety reasons and so everyone will enjoy the class.

Set up a plan for when children are not following the rules. Children who are unwilling to follow the rules in my cooking class are dismissed. I have one of the regular Sunday school teachers (who are usually participating in the cooking class) take them out of the kitchen. I have a two strikes, you're out policy—one warning and then you're out. This may sound strict, but you need to be strict in these situations. I remind the children that cooking in the church kitchen is a privilege. The privilege is taken away if you are not willing to respect me and others by following the rules.

2. LESS IS MORE. Keep in mind the cooking activity will probably take more time than you think, so always err in favor of doing less.

3. LESS IS STILL MORE. Don't try to work with too many children in the kitchen at a time. I've found I can manage two groups of six to eight children each, one after the other during the same church service. I wouldn't want many more than that. If you have larger groups in your situation, consider the activities in this book that can be adapted well for the classroom. These are the activities that require decorating, assembling, etc. You would then, most likely, set things up on a table in the classroom instead of using the kitchen.

4. EXPECT THE UNEXPECTED. Always have extra of everything—from paper cups to marshmallows and frosting.

5. THE EARLY (AND PREPARED) BIRD CATCHES THE WORM. Preheat your oven with plenty of time to spare so you are not waiting for this during cooking class. Have all your equipment lined up and ready with time to spare. Double-check what items you will need to bring from home. My rule of thumb is to bring just about everything from home, that way I know I will have it there. Pots and pans have a habit of disappearing from church kitchens from one week to the next, so it is hard to count on them for your purposes.

6. ALL THE COMFORTS OF HOME. Do as much pre-class preparation as you can at your own home. There are often other people using the church kitchen before, during, and after our cooking time (making coffee, etc.) so it is best for all if you take up less time and space in the church kitchen.

7. WATCH THE CLOCK. I designed these cooking activities based on the amount of time I thought most of you would be working with. If your cooking time is even more limited, there are ways to shave even more time off. For example, with the God Created The Heavens And The Earth activity (edible earth balls), you could make the blue and green cereal mixtures before cooking class. This way the children would simply need to assemble their own edible earth balls.

If time is very limited, look at the steps listed under each "Cooking Class" list, and see if any of these steps could be done ahead of time.

8. SHARE AND SHARE ALIKE. Children are so proud when they make something fabulous in the kitchen. They like to show their siblings or parents what they have made and possibly share it with them. When possible, plan this into your activities. For example, when you decorate star cookies, have each child decorate two or three. When you assemble the Jelly Bean Easter Prayers, let the children make one for each of their siblings. Children that don't have a sibling can make one for a parent, grandparent, or friend.

9. DESIGN YOUR COOKING ACTIVITIES FOR SUCCESS. There are little things you can do to help children feel successful in the kitchen. If eggs need to be separated, use an egg separator to assure that the yolk won't work its way into the egg white. When the children measure flour, have them do so over a jelly roll pan that can easily be cleaned should some spill out, rather than on the kitchen counter. Use good equipment such as air-cushion cookie sheets, thick, nonstick pots, etc. The cookies will be more likely not to burn, and the peanut brittle will be more likely to cook evenly.

10. DRESS FOR SUCCESS. You may want the children to come with an apron or old shirt from home that can be worn over their "Sunday best." Have them write their name on it with fabric paint so they can use it week after week.

11. LAST BUT NOT LEAST, CLEAN-UP. Given time constraints, you will most likely be the only one on the cleanup crew. You have so little time in the kitchen with the children as it is, it is likely you will need to send the children off for the rest of their Sunday school class while you do the cleanup. Still, this is an important component of cooking—one children need to be aware of. When time permits, have the children help with the cleanup. Remind them that while cooking and eating may be the fun part, cleanup is the necessary part.

MAKE THE MOST OF YOUR CAPTIVE AUDIENCE

1. DON'T FORGET TO TEACH THEM SOMETHING ABOUT THE BIBLE. Let's face it. Cooking and eating food are great. But the whole point to these cooking activities is to get the kids thinking, to get them interested in the Bible, and to teach them more about what it means to be a Christian. Plan time during your cooking class or during regular Sunday school time to go over the message and scripture that correspond to each cooking adventure.

2. MAKE THE MOST OF YOUR CAPTIVE AUDIENCE. When your cooking class has a little down time in the kitchen, perhaps while you are all waiting a few minutes for something to melt or bake, take advantage of it. This is when I usually take time to read the applicable scripture and discuss the general message with the children. As long as I keep my messages brief, I find the children are usually very interested in what I have to say at this point.

3. DON'T FORGET TO PLEASE THE PRIEST OR PASTOR. It is a good idea to run these activities and lesson plans by your priest or pastor just to make sure he or she is comfortable with your plans. I make it a habit to share the fruits of our kitchen labor with the pastors (who are always happy to help taste) and anyone else who happens by the kitchen. Not only is this good P.R. for your cooking efforts, it's just a nice thing to do.

4. TRY THIS AT HOME. If your cooking class participants are anything like the ones I've worked with, they will want copies of the recipes to take home. And you will want them to have the general messages and copies of the scripture to take home. So why not invest in a copy of *Bible Lessons in the Kitchen* for each of the children in your cooking class? Perhaps there is a church fund that can contribute towards the cost, or perhaps interested parents can purchase the book themselves. This way, the children can make these recipes again and again.

BIBLE LESSONS
IN THE
KITCHEN

HONORING PARENTS AND GRANDPARENTS

God commands us to respect our parents, to listen to their words and follow the rules they set before us as we grow up. This is so important to God, that he made it one of his 10 Commandments (Exodus 20:12). One way to honor our parents and grandparents is to thank them for all their love and guidance. Here are a couple food gift activities that can be made to give thanks to our parents and grandparents.

EXODUS 20:12
Honor your father and your mother, so that you may
live long in the land the Lord your God is giving you.

PROVERBS 23:22
Listen to your father, who gave you life,
and do not despise your mother when she is old.

COUNTRY RECIPE PANCAKE SYRUP

EQUIPMENT

large, heavy saucepan
wooden spoon
2 or 4 cup measure (liquid)
1 cup measure (dry)

measuring spoons
9 8-ounce jars (or 18 4-ounce jars)
  with lids

INGREDIENTS

3 cups water
9 cups dark brown sugar, packed

1 1/2 teaspoons ground cinnamon
2 tablespoons vanilla extract

TEACHER PREP

1. Set out all the ingredients and equipment.

COOKING CLASS

1. One of the children can measure the water and pour it into the saucepan. Wait for the water to boil.

2. While you are waiting for the water to boil, several children can measure the brown sugar and put it into a large bowl.

3. Another child can measure the cinnamon and add it to the bowl with brown sugar; stir well.

4. Once the water begins to boil, reduce heat to medium-low and add sugar and cinnamon.

5. Stir constantly, until sugar is completely dissolved (about 5 minutes).

6. Two children can each measure a tablespoon of vanilla extract, then pour it into the mixture; stir well.

7. An adult can ladle the hot syrup into jars with lids, filling 2/3 or 3/4 full.

Makes approximately 7 cups pancake syrup; enough syrup for about 9 or 10 jars. Per tablespoon of pancake syrup: 83 calories, 0 protein, 21 g carbohydrate, 0 fat, 8 mg sodium.

HOMEMADE LEMON CURD

Lemon curd can be served with biscuits, muffins, or toast or use it with desserts such as angel food cake, cheesecake, cookies, etc.

EQUIPMENT

large, heavy saucepan
  (preferably nonstick)
zesting tool
wooden spoon

measuring cups
4 cup measure
plastic knives
8 to 10 4-ounce containers

INGREDIENTS

2 cups sugar
1/4 cup Wondra quick-mixing flour
2 tablespoons finely shredded
  lemon peel (peel from about
  4 of the lemons)

2 cups lemon juice (about 10 lemons)
4 tablespoons butter or margarine
4 eggs
1/2 cup egg substitute

TEACHER PREP

1. Set out large, heavy saucepan.

2. Six of the lemons can be cut in half (horizontally). The other four can be cut in half after the children take off the peel with the zester (see cooking class below).

COOKING CLASS

1. Get a couple of children going on removing the lemon peel from 4 lemons with a zesting tool. The lemon zest should then be finely chopped with a knife (an adult may want to do this) and added to the saucepan. These lemons can be cut in half and given to the children squeezing out the juice (see number 4 below).

2. Another child can measure the sugar and pour it into the saucepan.

3. A child can measure the Wondra flour and add it to the saucepan.

4. A couple of the children can start squeezing the juice from three of the lemons that have been cut in half (they can squeeze them over a 4-cup measure). After 2 cups of juice has been collected and the seeds have been fished out, it can be added to the saucepan.

5. A child can cut the butter into small pieces using a plastic knife and add the butter to the saucepan.

6. An older child can crack eggs in a mixing bowl. Measure and add egg substitute to the eggs and beat them together briefly. Add egg mixture to saucepan.

7. Someone can stir up the ingredients in the saucepan.

8. Cook mixture over medium-low heat for about 8 minutes or until it thickens and coats the back of the spoon. Stir constantly and do not let mixture boil—if the mixture starts to boil, reduce heat to a simmer.

9. Pour into gift containers. Makes about 4 cups of lemon curd or will fill 8 or 10 4-ounce containers. Cover with lids and refrigerate no longer than 2 months.

Makes 4 cups
Per tablespoon: 38 calories, .6 g protein, 7 g carbohydrate, 1 g fat, 15 mg cholesterol, 15 mg sodium. Calories from fat: 24 percent.

BRINGING GOD'S LIGHT HOME

God is light. Just as the one bright star shone over the manger when Christ was born, God's light continues to shine all around us.

1 JOHN 1:5
This is the message we have heard from him and declare to you:
God is light; in him there is no darkness at all.

LUKE 2:8-12
And there were shepherds living out in the fields nearby, keeping watch over their flocks at night. An angel of the Lord appeared to them, and the glory of the Lord shone around them, and they were terrified. But the angel said to them, "Do not be afraid. I bring you good news of great joy that will be for all the people. Today in the town of David a Savior has been born to you, he is Christ the Lord. This will be a sign to you: You will find a baby wrapped in strips of cloth and lying in a manger."

MERINGUE STAR COOKIES

EQUIPMENT

electric mixer and mixing bowl
1 large or 2 small cookie sheets
parchment paper
measuring spoons

measuring cups
decorator's bag or cookie press
with large star tip

INGREDIENTS

2 egg whites
1 teaspoon vanilla extract
1/4 teaspoon cream of tartar

1/2 cup sugar
assorted sprinkles

TEACHER PREP

1. Add egg whites to mixing bowl and let stand at room temperature for at least 1 hour.

2. Line 1 large or 2 small cookie sheets with parchment paper or foil. Set aside.

3. Preheat oven to 300 degrees.

COOKING CLASS

1. A child can add vanilla to mixing bowl.

2. A child can add cream of tartar to mixing bowl.

3. Beat with an electric mixer on medium speed till soft peaks form (tips curl).

4. Have one of the children measure the sugar, then gradually add in the sugar while continuing to beat the egg white mixture, 1 tablespoon at a time. (You can have eight children line up, each adding a tablespoon.)

5. Beat on high speed till stiff peaks form (tips stand straight) and sugar is almost dissolved.

6. Spoon meringue mixture into the decorator's bag fitted with a large star tip (1/2-inch opening) or add meringue to a cookie press and use the star disc. Pipe 2 to 2 1/2-inch wide stars about 1 1/2 inches apart onto prepared cookie sheets.

7. The children can decorate the stars with assorted sprinkles and decorations, if desired.

8. Bake in a preheated oven about 15 minutes or until cookies just start to turn brown. Turn off oven and let cookie dry in oven with door closed for 15 to 30 minutes. Bend parchment paper to remove meringues.

Makes about 20 star cookies.
Per cookie: 21 calories, .4 g protein, 5 g carbohydrate, O fat, O cholesterol, 6 mg sodium. Calories from fat: O.

RESISTING TEMPTATION

The serpent appears several times in the Bible. For example, in Genesis 3:1-5 the serpent is a tricky wild animal that tries to talk Adam and Eve out of obeying God's wishes. In life there are many "serpents"—people trying to talk us out of obeying God and his commandments. The devil even tried to tempt Jesus (Luke 4:1-13) but Jesus held fast to the words and ways of God and eventually the devil left him.

GENESIS 3:1-5

Now the serpent was more crafty than any of the wild animals the Lord God had made. He said to the woman (Eve), "Did God really say, 'You must not eat from any tree in the garden'?"

The woman said to the serpent, "We may eat fruit from the trees in the garden, but God did say, 'You must not eat fruit from the tree that is in the middle of the garden, and you must not touch it, or you will die.'"

"You will not surely die," the serpent said to the woman. "For God knows that when you eat of it your eyes will be opened, and you will be like God, knowing good and evil."

CHOCOLATE SERPENT COOKIES

EQUIPMENT

electric mixer

cookie sheet

mixing bowl or 4 cup measure

INGREDIENTS

6 tablespoons margarine or butter

6 tablespoons fat-free cream cheese

3/4 cup sugar

1/4 cup egg substitute

2 teaspoons vanilla extract

1 3/4 cups flour

1/4 cup cocoa

1/4 teaspoon baking powder

nonstick cooking spray

powdered sugar

milk

colored sugar

snake eyes: mini M & Ms, whole
    cloves, or red candies

TEACHER PREP

1. In large mixing bowl, beat butter and cream cheese with electric mixer on medium speed about 30 seconds or till blended. Add sugar and beat till fluffy. Add egg substitute and vanilla and beat well.

2. In medium mixing bowl or 4-cup measure, stir together flour, cocoa, and baking powder.

3. Gradually add the flour mixture to the butter mixture, beating well. Divide dough in half. Cover and chill about 30 minutes or till dough is easy to handle.

4. Preheat oven to 375 degrees. Coat cookie sheets with cooking spray.

COOKING CLASS

1. Generously dust working surface with powdered sugar. Have each child take a couple tablespoons of the dough and roll it into a 10-inch rope. Coil the rope into a circle, then bend back the end of the rope for the serpent's head, or bending the rope left and right to make a slithering serpent. Or a more 3 dimensional serpent can be made by coiling the rope around in smaller and smaller circles (coiling up).

2. Brush serpents with milk and sprinkle them with colored sugar.

3. Bake for 8 to 10 minutes or until just lightly browned.

Makes about 24 serpents.

Per cookie: 90 calories, 2 g protein, 14 g carbohydrate, 3 g fat, .6 g fiber, 8 mg cholesterol, 59 mg sodium. Calories from fat: 30 percent.

LEARNING PERSEVERANCE

To persevere is to hold on tight to a purpose, or to keep working at a chore even when it gets a little difficult. We need to hold on tight to our faith and love for God. Making cashew brittle is a somewhat tiring process. Just when it seems like you can't stir the pot another minute, the brittle is ready, and it is time to add the baking soda and vanilla and pour it into the prepared pan. The result of all your stirring and perseverance? Fabulous cashew brittle that can be shared with others.

GALATIANS 6:7-9

A man reaps what he sows. The one who sows to please his sinful nature, from that nature will reap destruction; the one who sows to please the Spirit, from the Spirit will reap eternal life. Let us not become weary in doing good, for at the proper time we will reap a harvest if we do not give up.

2 THESSALONIANS 3:11-13

We hear that some among you are idle. They are not busy; they are busybodies. In the name of the Lord Jesus Christ, we command and urge such people to settle down and earn the bread they eat. And as for you, brothers, never tire of doing what is right.

CASHEW BRITTLE

Because this food activity requires stirring hot liquid, it is best for older children. Younger children can help while an adult stirs.

EQUIPMENT

large nonstick saucepan
wooden spoon
candy thermometer
2 cup measure

measuring spoons
1 jelly roll pan (11 x 15 x 1 inch)
sandwich bags or plastic wrap
    and ribbon

INGREDIENTS

2 cups sugar
1 cup water
2/3 cup light corn syrup
1 3/4 cups cashews

nonstick cooking spray
4 teaspoons baking soda
1 tablespoon butter
1 1/2 teaspoons pure vanilla extract

TEACHER PREP

1. Get all of the ingredients and equipment out and ready to go.

2. About 8 minutes before the children are expected to arrive in the kitchen, start measuring the sugar, water, and corn syrup into the large saucepan. Bring them to a boil over medium heat. Continue boiling and stirring until it reaches 230 degrees on the candy thermometer. Ideally it will reach 230 degrees after the children arrive so they can watch this step.

COOKING CLASS

1. Once the class arrives, they can help you keep an eye on the temperature on the candy thermometer. Perhaps an older child can hold it in place (not hitting bottom of pan but well into the mixture) while the adult, or an older child, continues to stir.

2. One of the children needs to measure the cashews in a 2-cup measure.

3. Once the mixture hits 230 degrees, have one of the children pour the cashews into the hot mixture. The adult or older child needs to continue to cook and stir the mixture continuously until the syrup turns a golden color. The smell of the cashews will be very noticeable at this point. (This takes about 8 minutes after the cashews are added.)

4. While the class is waiting, one of the children can coat the bottom and sides of the jelly roll pan with cooking spray. Another child can measure the baking soda, someone else can get the butter ready, and another can measure the vanilla extract.

5. Once the mixture turns a golden color, immediately remove the saucepan from the heat and the adult can stir while children add the baking soda, butter, and vanilla. Stir until blended. An adult can pour the mixture into the prepared jelly roll pan. The mixture is very hot so it is best if an adult spreads the mixture with a wooden spoon to reach the sides. Once the brittle hardens (about 10 or so minutes), children can break it into pieces. The children can put a couple pieces of brittle in a sandwich bag or some plastic wrap, tie with ribbon, and give as a treat to someone they know.

Makes about 12 ounces of cashew brittle.
Per ounce of brittle: 304 calories, 3 g protein, 54 g carbohydrate, 10 g fat, .6 g fiber, 2 mg cholesterol, 35 mg sodium. Calories from fat: 29 percent.

FINDING SUPPORT IN GOD'S WORD

The staff is mentioned often in the Bible; it's mentioned in Psalm 23 as well as with Moses and his staff. A staff is a stick used to lean on and is also referred to as a rod used by shepherds. Psalm 23 brings many people comfort. This is an excellent psalm for school-age children to memorize and keep in their hearts and minds.

PSALM 23 (A PSALM OF DAVID)

The Lord is my shepherd, I shall not be in want.
He makes me lie down in green pastures,
He leads me beside quiet waters, he restores my soul.
He guides me in paths of righteousness for his name's sake.
Even though I walk through the valley of the shadow of death,
I will fear no evil, for you are with me;
your rod and your staff, they comfort me.
You prepare a table before me in the presence of my enemies.
You anoint my head with oil; my cup overflows.
Surely goodness and love will follow me all the days of my life,
and I will dwell in the house of the Lord forever.

CHICKEN STICKS

EQUIPMENT

large saucepan
2 medium bowls
4 zip-type bags

9 x 13-inch baking pan
small microwave-safe custard cup
(or small saucepan)

INGREDIENTS

6 chicken breasts, skinless,
and boneless
4 cups low-sodium chicken broth
1/4 cup low-fat milk
1 egg or 1/4 cup egg substitute
1 cup flour
1 teaspoon garlic powder

1 teaspoon paprika
1/2 teaspoon poultry seasoning
3/4 teaspoon black pepper
1 teaspoon salt
1 tablespoon butter-flavored
shortening
nonstick cooking spray

TEACHER PREP

1. The night before or several hours before cooking class, cut chicken breasts on the diagonal into strips (about 6 strips per breast). Add chicken strips and chicken broth to large saucepan. Bring broth to low boil, reduce heat to simmer, cover pan, and simmer until chicken is cooked throughout (about 30 minutes). Drain chicken strips and let cool in refrigerator.

2. Blend milk and egg in one of the bowls; set aside.

3. Combine flour, garlic powder, paprika, poultry seasoning, black pepper, and salt in the other bowl. Distribute flour mixture evenly into the plastic bags.

4. Coat 9 x 13-inch pan with 1/2 tablespoon shortening. Melt the remaining 1/2 tablespoon shortening in the custard cup in the microwave or in the saucepan on the stove, and set aside.

5. Preheat oven to 350 degrees.

COOKING CLASS

1. Have children wash their hands before starting. Washing hands before and during cooking is always important, but it is particularly important when meat is involved. Although this recipe is designed so that the children will not be working with *raw* chicken, washing hands before cooking is nonetheless important.

2. Demonstrate for the children how to shake chicken strips (about 4 at a time) in flour mixture, then dip chicken strips in milk/egg mixture, and finally shake chicken a second time in flour mixture to coat well.

3. Have each child coat about 4 chicken strips each in the flour and egg mixture then place chicken strips in prepared baking pan.

4. The teacher or the children can spray the tops of chicken strips with cooking spray and drizzle the remaining shortening evenly over chicken.

5. The teacher can now bake chicken strips for about 10 minutes. Turn strips over and bake 10 minutes more.

Makes about 36 strips (12 servings, if 3 strips each).
Per serving: 111 calories, 15 g protein, 6 g carbohydrates, 2.5 g fat, .3 g fiber, 52 mg cholesterol, 190 mg sodium. Calories from fat: 20 percent.

COMING TOGETHER IN HARMONY

We are all part of the body of Christ. If we work together we can do magnificent things. Alone, we have two balls of bread dough. But together, we have a wonderful loaf of cinnamon pull-apart bread.

1 CORINTHIANS 12:27
Now you are the body of Christ, and each one of you is a part of it.

CINNAMON PULL-APART BREAD

EQUIPMENT

6 small bowls
small saucepan

large loaf pan

INGREDIENTS

2 tablespoons ground cinnamon
1/2 cup sugar
4 tablespoons butter

2 cans Pillsbury Crusty French Loaf dough (you will need one can for every 10 children)
nonstick cooking spray

TEACHER PREP

1. Blend cinnamon with sugar. Divide this mixture into three small bowls.

2. Melt butter in saucepan or using microwave. Divide into three small bowls.

3. Divide each loaf of dough into 5 slices then cut each slice into fourths. You should have about 20 pieces of dough (providing a group of 10 children with 2 pieces each).

4. Preheat oven to 350 degrees. Coat the loaf pan with cooking spray.

COOKING CLASS

1. Give each child approximately 2 pieces of bread dough.

2. Have the children form three lines. In front of each line place one bowl of melted butter and one bowl of cinnamon-sugar. In the middle of the kitchen counter, place the empty loaf pan.

3. Show the children how to dip each ball of dough first in the butter, then roll around in the cinnamon-sugar, and then place in the loaf pan. Repeat with second ball of dough.

4. Once the loaf pan is full of dough balls, bake for about 25 minutes.

5. Children can go back to Sunday school for the rest of their lessons and activities. By the time church is over, the bread will be ready!

Makes 20 samples.
Per sample: 77 calories, 1.5 g protein, 12 g carbohydrate, 2.5 g fat, 6 mg cholesterol, 120 mg sodium. Calories from fat: 32 percent.

PUTTING ON A HAPPY FACE

Be a happy, positive person. As a Christian, you are a messenger to others. Set a good example. Try not to dwell on anger, but find comfort in God's love.

PROVERBS 3:3-4
Let love and faithfulness never leave you; bind them around your neck, write them on the tablet of your heart. Then you will win favor and a good name in the sight of God and man.

M & M COOKIES

EQUIPMENT

mixer

mixing bowls

cookie scoop

cookie sheets

2 small bowls

sugar

several glasses with flat bottoms

M & Ms

raisins

TEACHER PREP

1. Prepare a batch of sugar cookie dough and/or a batch of chocolate cookie dough (recipes follow).

2. Scoop cookie dough with cookie scoop and place on cookie sheets that have been coated with cooking spray.

3. Put some water in one bowl and some sugar in another.

4. Preheat oven according to recipe.

COOKING CLASS

1. Have students dip the bottom of a glass in water then in sugar. Then have the students press the sugar coated bottom onto one of the cookie dough lumps on the cookie sheet to flatten nicely. Dip the glass bottom in the sugar again and press onto another lump of cookie dough. Repeat until all cookie dough lumps are flattened.

2. Students can now make faces (happy faces for God) in the cookie dough using M & M's and raisins.

3. Bake for about 8 to 10 minutes. Since this cookie dough is made with 50 percent less fat it is important not to overbake them (under-cook them slightly to maintain a soft and chewy texture). Remove with spatula and let cool on wire rack.

SUGAR COOKIE DOUGH

INGREDIENTS

1/2 cup butter or margarine, softened
1/2 cup fat-free cream cheese
1 1/2 cups + 3 tablespoons sugar
1 egg and 1 egg white
1 teaspoon vanilla extract

2 3/4 cups all-purpose flour
2 teaspoons cream of tartar
1 teaspoon baking soda
1/4 teaspoon salt
nonstick cooking spray

PREPARATION

1. Use a mixer to blend the butter with the cream cheese. Mix in 1 1/2 cups of the sugar and beat until smooth. (Place remaining sugar in bowl for dipping the glass.) Add the eggs and vanilla. Stir in the flour, cream of tartar, baking soda, and salt. Refrigerate for at least an hour.

2. Preheat oven to 400 degrees. Use cookie scoop to place dough on cookie sheets coated with cooking spray.

Makes 3 dozen large cookies.
Per serving: 98 calories, 1.7 g protein, 16.7 g carbohydrate, 2.8 g fat, 13 mg cholesterol, .3 g fiber, 85 mg sodium. Calories from fat: 25 percent.

CHEWY CHOCOLATE COOKIE DOUGH

INGREDIENTS

nonstick cooking spray
5 tablespoons butter, softened
7 tablespoons fat-free cream cheese
2 cups sugar
1 egg
1/4 cup egg substitute

1 tablespoon vanilla extract
2 cups all-purpose flour
3/4 cup unsweetened cocoa
1 teaspoon baking soda
1/2 teaspoon salt

PREPARATION

1. Preheat the oven to 350 degrees. Coat 2 cookie sheets with cooking spray.

2. In a large bowl, cream the butter and cream cheese together. Add the sugar and beat until creamy. Add the egg, egg substitute, and vanilla and beat until smooth. Combine the flour, cocoa, baking soda, and salt in a medium bowl. Add to the butter mixture and beat until blended. Use cookie scoop to place dough on cookie sheets.

Makes 2 1/2 dozen cookies.
Per cookie: 112 calories, 2.5 g protein, 21 g carbohydrate, 2.5 g fat, 1 g fiber, 12 mg cholesterol, 69 mg sodium. Calories from fat: 19 percent.

LOOKING ON THE BRIGHT SIDE

Flat breads are probably the oldest form of bread in the world. The flat breads that use yeast (like pita bread) originated in the Mediterranean where the practice of using yeast to add air to bread first began.

When Moses led the Israelites out of Egypt, the people had little warning that it was time to pack up and leave their homes. They had no time to add yeast to their kneading troughs of bread dough. And so they took their troughs of unleavened dough with them on their journey, and later, they baked their yeastless cakes of dough.

Sometimes things don't always work out the way we think they should. Instead of being disappointed and angry, we can look for the best in the situation. Ask yourself, "What lesson have I learned because of this?" The result may not be what you expected, but some good may still come out of it. And in the case of flat bread (pita bread), it may not be the fluffy bread we are used to, but the result is still delicious!

EXODUS 12:39
With the dough they had brought from Egypt, they baked cakes of unleavened bread. The dough was without yeast because they had been driven out of Egypt and did not have time to prepare food for themselves.

PITA BREAD

EQUIPMENT

2 pound loaf bread machine
baking sheets

butter, jelly, cheese, or peanut
butter (optional)

TEACHER PREP

1. About 2 hours before you need the dough, add pita bread ingredients to bread machine (see recipe below). Program the bread machine for the "dough" cycle. This should take about 1 hour and 40 minutes. If you need to make two batches of dough because you have more than 10 children in your cooking class, you can make two batches simultaneously using two bread machines or you can keep the first batch of dough in the refrigerator while you make the second. It will take approximately 3 hours and 20 minutes to make two batches of dough. You can always make the dough the night before and pop it in the refrigerator until morning.

2. Set out baking sheets. Have a large surface or cutting board covered well with some flour. Preheat oven to 500 degrees.

3. Divide each batch of flattened dough into about 10 pieces.

COOKING CLASS

1. Give each child a piece of pita bread dough and have them roll the dough on the floured surface to coat well with flour. Show them how to flatten and roll each ball of dough into a circle about 6 inches wide and 1/8 inch thick, using the palms of their hands.

2. Have the children put their pita bread pancakes on a baking sheet and place the baking sheets on the lowest rack of the oven. Close the oven door (do not peek) for exactly 1 minute. Then move the baking sheets to a rack higher in the oven and cook 3 to 7 minutes or until pitas have blown up and are lightly browned.

3. Serve the hot pitas with butter, jelly, cheese, or peanut butter, if desired.

PITA BREAD DOUGH

2 cups water
1 tablespoon sugar
1 tablespoon salt

1 tablespoon active dry yeast
6 cups unbleached all-purpose flour
   (or 1 packet)

PREPARATION

1. Put all ingredients in bread machine in the order recommended by your bread machine manual. (I usually add the water, then sugar, then flour. I make a well in the center of the flour and place the yeast there. I then pour the salt into one corner of the machine.)

2. Set machine to "dough cycle" (it rises only once and then the machine stops). This should take about 1 hour and 40 minutes. Knock the dough down if the machine hasn't already done so and divide the dough into about 10 pieces. Preheat oven to 500 degrees.

3. Flatten and roll each piece into a circle about 6 inches wide and 1/8 inch thick on a well floured surface. Place pitas on baking sheets. When oven is good and hot, place baking sheet on the bottom of the oven (or on lowest rack). Close the oven door (do not peek) for exactly 1 minute. Move baking sheets to a high rack in oven and continue to bake 3 to 7 minutes or until pitas have blown up and are lightly browned.

Makes about 10 pita breads.
Per pita: 280 calories, 8 g protein, 59 g carbohydrate, .8 g fat, 2.5 g fiber,
0 cholesterol, 640 mg sodium. Calories from fat: 3 percent.

THE LESSON OF ADAM & EVE

What God created is good, and God created you. You are beautiful and you are good. There are some things that God created but that he wants us to stay away from for our own safety—like poisonous plants or grizzly bears—just as God warned Adam and Eve to stay away from the tree of knowledge of good and evil (the forbidden fruit).

GENESIS 2:16-17
And the Lord God commanded the man, "You are free to eat from any tree in the garden; but you must not eat from the tree of the knowledge of good and evil, for when you eat of it you will surely die."

ADAM & EVE FAST APPLE PIE

This recipe is a cross between apple pie and apple cake. The taste is similar to apple pie, but there are no crusts, only a cake-like batter. This is the perfect recipe to use for a lesson on Genesis and the Adam & Eve scripture since this pie seems a bit naked without a crust and it features the forbidden fruit—the apple.

EQUIPMENT

pie plate
mixing bowl
mixer or wooden spoon
apple slicers

plastic knives
vanilla ice cream or light whipped
   topping (optional)

INGREDIENTS

nonstick cooking spray
1/4 cup egg substitute
1/2 cup brown sugar
1/2 cup white sugar
1 1/2 teaspoons vanilla extract
1/2 teaspoon almond extract

pinch salt
1/2 teaspoon ground cinnamon
1/2 cup flour
1 teaspoon baking powder
3 apples
1/2 cup chopped pecans (optional)

TEACHER PREP

1. Preheat oven to 350 degrees.

2. Coat pie plates with cooking spray.

3. Place egg substitute, sugars, extracts, salt, cinnamon, flour, and baking powder in mixing bowl and beat until well blended.

4. Set out apples, several apple slicers, and plastic knives.

COOKING CLASS

Because this recipe takes about 25 minutes to bake, have the children come to the kitchen first then they can go to Sunday school while the apple pies bake.

1. Show the children how to use the apple slicers to core and split the apples into large wedges.

2. The children can now use the plastic knives to split the wedges into thinner slices.

3. Have the children drop the apple slices and pecans into the batter. One of the children can stir the apple slices into the batter, then another can pour the mixture into the prepared pie plate.

4. The teacher now bakes the pies for 23 to 25 minutes or until the edges are lightly browned. Serve with light vanilla ice cream or light whipped topping if desired.

Makes 9 servings.
Per serving: 144 calories, 1.5 g protein, 35 g carbohydrate, .3 g fat, 1.5 g fiber, 0 cholesterol, 69 mg sodium. Calories from fat: 2 percent.

APPLE PIZZA
(an alternate recipe for home)

DOUGH

1 1/2 cups warm low-fat milk
1/2 cup brown sugar
1 egg, slightly beaten,
  with 1/4 cup egg substitute
1 tablespoon canola oil
1 tablespoon salt

2 teaspoons cinnamon
2 cups whole wheat flour
4 cups unbleached all-purpose flour
1 tablespoon active dry yeast
  (or 1 packet)

3 large or 4 medium apples
3/4 cup pecan halves or pieces
2 teaspoons cinnamon

TOPPING

1/2 cup brown sugar
1/2 cup raisins (optional)

GLAZE

1 cup powdered sugar
2 tablespoons milk

1 teaspoon vanilla extract

PREPARATION
IF USING BREAD MACHINE:

1. Add dough ingredients to bread machine in the order recommended in your bread machine manual. Set bread machine to "dough" setting and press start (this will usually take about an hour and 40 minutes to complete).

IF MAKING THE DOUGH BY HAND OR USING A MIXER:

1. Dissolve a tablespoon of the sugar and the yeast in the warm milk. Beat in the egg, egg substitute, and oil. Add the remaining brown sugar, salt, and cinnamon. Mix in the flour, a cup at a time.

2. Turn dough onto a floured surface and knead until smooth and elastic. Let the dough rise in a greased covered bowl while you make the topping.

FOR BOTH BREAD MACHINE AND BY HAND:

1. Preheat oven to 400 degrees. Thinly slice the apples (peel them first if you prefer them peeled). Grind or chop the nuts. Add the nuts to a medium bowl and stir in cinnamon, brown sugar, and raisins if desired; set aside.

2. Divide dough into 2 pieces. Using well floured hands, press each piece onto a lightly greased 12-inch pizza pan (or similar sized pan). Cover the dough with a layer of sliced apples. Sprinkle the sugar and pecan mixture over the top of each pizza.

3. Bake for 10 minutes, then reduce the temperature to 350 degrees and bake 10 or 15 minutes more. Once cooled slightly, blend the glaze ingredients until smooth and drizzle over the apple pizzas.

YOUR BODY IS YOUR TEMPLE

Your body is a gift from God. When you take good care of it, by eating healthfully and exercising often, you honor God. One of the best ways to improve your health is by eating at least 5 servings of fruits and vegetables every day. In our busy lives of fast food and microwave meals, fruits and vegetables are often left behind. We need to make an extra effort to eat fruits and vegetables.

1 CORINTHIANS 6:19-20
Do you not know that your body is a temple of the Holy Spirit, who is in you, whom you have received from God? You are not your own; you were bought at a price. Therefore honor God with your body.

FRUIT KABOBS

EQUIPMENT

5 serving bowls   10 bamboo skewers

INGREDIENTS PER 10 KABOB

5 kiwi   2 1/2 cups watermelon cubes
30 cantaloupe balls   (about 1 small watermelon)
  (about 2 cantaloupes)   2 1/2 cups seedless grapes
2 1/2 cups banana slices
  (about 3 bananas)

Note: other fruits (such as canned pineapple chunks) can be substituted for the above fruits if they are not available.

TEACHER PREP

1. Cut each kiwi into 4 slices, peel the slices and put in a bowl.

2. Make about 30 melon balls from seeded cantaloupe halves and put in a bowl.

3. Peel and slice bananas and put in a bowl.

4. Cut seeded watermelon into cubes and put in a bowl.

5. Wash grapes, pull from stems, and put in a bowl.

COOKING CLASS

1. Have children make fruit kabobs by threading an assortment of fruit onto the bamboo skewers.

Makes 10 kabobs.
Per kabob: 113 calories, 1.5 g protein, 28 g carbohydrate, 1 g fat, 2 g fiber, 0 cholesterol, 8 mg sodium. Calories from fat: 6 percent.

Note: a serving of this fruit snack also includes lots of important vitamins and minerals: 19% Recommended Daily Allowance (RDA) for vitamin A, 10% for B1, 24% for B6, 14% for folacin, 110% for vitamin C, 12% for vitamin E, 17% for iron, 12% for magnesium, and 26% for potassium.

SALAD BAR

Make a salad bar by putting each salad ingredient in its own serving bowl and putting all the bowls in a line.

EQUIPMENT

many serving bowls of various sizes
lettuce spinner (optional)
can opener
strainer
grater

peeler (optional)
plastic knives
disposable bowls or paper plates
plastic forks

INGREDIENTS

a bag or a bunch or two
   of spinach leaves
two heads leaf lettuce
3 cups canned garbanzo
   or kidney beans
3 carrots
1 large bunch broccoli
2 cucumbers
1 container (about 2 cups)
   cherry tomatoes

2 different types of bottled salad
   dressing (preferably with 5 grams fat
   or less per 2 tablespoon serving,
   such as Wishbone Olive Oil
   Vinaigrette)
reduced fat croutons (optional)
roasted sunflower seeds (optional)
grated reduced-calorie sharp
   cheddar cheese (optional)

TEACHER PREP

1. Wash and shred lettuce. Place in large bowl. Wash spinach and place in another bowl.

2. Open canned beans; drain, and rinse well. Place in serving bowl.

3. Wash whole carrots, broccoli, cucumber, and cherry tomatoes.

4. Set out serving bowls or plates, plastic forks, and salad dressing.

COOKING CLASS

1. One of the older children can grate the carrots then place in serving bowl.

2. One of the older children can peel the cucumber (if desired), and cut into thin slices using a plastic knife.

3. One of the children can break the broccoli bunch into smaller florets, and place in serving bowl.

4. One of the children can cut the cherry tomatoes in half using a plastic knife.

5. One of the children can spin the lettuce with the salad spinner or pat it dry with a towel. Put lettuce back in large serving bowl.

6. Another child can dry the spinach.

7. A child can pour the croutons into one of the serving bowls. Sunflower seeds and grated cheese can also be placed in serving bowls.

8. After the salad bar is ready to go, the children can form a line and proceed through the salad bar adding what they want to make a healthy salad!

Makes about 12 salads.

Per salad (with 1/2 cup of lettuce, 1/2 cup spinach, 1/4 cup raw carrot, 1/4 cup broccoli pieces, 6 slices cucumber, 1/4 cup beans, 2 cherry tomatoes, and 2 tablespoons olive oil vinaigrette): 171 calories, 5.5 g protein, 26 g carbohydrate, 6 g fat, 5.5 g fiber, 0 cholesterol, 473 mg sodium. Calories from fat: 31 percent.

Note: a serving of this salad also includes lots of important vitamins and minerals: 135% RDA for vitamin A, 11% for B1, 12% for B2, 7% for B3, 29% for B6, 76% for folacin, 77% for vitamin C, 20% for vitamin E, 7% for calcium, 17% for iron, 21% for magnesium, and 30% for potassium.

STRAWBERRY-ORANGE SMOOTHIE

EQUIPMENT

blender or food processor
1 cup measure
2 cup measure

1/2 cup measuring cup
8 paper cups

INGREDIENTS

1 heaping cup light vanilla ice cream or frozen yogurt
2 cups sliced strawberries

2 cups orange juice
1/2 cup nonfat dry milk (if desired)

TEACHER PREP

1. Set out equipment.

2. If time is limited, wash and slice strawberries (otherwise the children can slice them using plastic knives).

COOKING CLASS

1. A child can measure the ice cream and add it to the blender.

2. Another child can measure and add the strawberries to the blender.

3. A third child can measure and add the orange juice to the blender.

4. Another child can measure and add the nonfat dry milk to the blender, if desired.

5. An adult or older child can puree the mixture in the blender. Pour mixture into paper cups.

Makes about 8 servings.
Per serving: 80 calories, 2.8 g protein, 15 g carbohydrate, 1.3 g fat, 1 g fiber, 7 mg cholesterol, 32 mg sodium. Calories from fat: 15 percent.

Note: a serving of this smoothie also includes lots of important vitamins and minerals: 13% RDA for vitamin A, 15% for B1, 18% for B2, 8% for B6, 16% for B12, 31% for folacin, 183% for vitamin C, 14% for calcium, 11% for magnesium, and 26% for potassium.

SHARING WHAT WE HAVE

Agape is a Greek word meaning God's love is unconditional. This "Agape feast" reminds us to share what we have. Communion started more as a potluck, with everyone bringing some food to share with others.

ACTS 2:44-47

All the believers were together and had everything in common. Selling their possessions and goods, they gave to anyone as he had need. Every day they continued to meet together in the temple courts. They broke bread in their homes and ate together with glad and sincere hearts, praising God and enjoying the favor of all the people. And the Lord added to their number daily those who were being saved.

TEACHER PREP

1. Decide which and how many muffin recipes you will be making. Then read each particular recipe (below) to follow instructions further.

2. Preheat oven to 350 or 400 degrees, depending on which recipe you make.

3. If there are many children involved with this activity, you can have the children form groups with each group making a different type of muffin.

4. If time is limited or you are working with younger children, you might consider measuring out all of the ingredients beforehand.

5. After the class has baked their muffins, baskets can be lined with cloth napkins. The children can fill each basket with a different type of muffin, and the muffins can be served following church if desired.

LEMONADE MUFFINS

EQUIPMENT

muffin pans

mixer and mixing bowl

measuring cups

zesting tool

measuring spoons

medium sized bowl

toothpicks or forks

INGREDIENTS

nonstick cooking spray

3 tablespoons butter, softened

1/3 cup nonfat cream cheese

1 cup sugar

1 egg

1/4 cup egg substitute

juice and finely chopped lemon
 zest of 1 lemon

1 1/2 cups flour

1 teaspoon baking powder

1/2 teaspoon salt

1/2 cup 1% low-fat milk

LEMONADE SYRUP TOPPING:

juice and finely chopped lemon
 zest of 2 lemons

1/3 cup sugar

TEACHER PREP

1. Preheat oven to 350 degrees. Coat muffin pan with cooking spray.

2. Blend butter and cream cheese together with mixer. Cream butter mixture and sugar together with mixer. Beat in egg. Beat in egg substitute. Beat in juice and lemon zest of 1 lemon (about 3 tablespoons juice and 1 teaspoon finely chopped lemon zest).

3. In another bowl, blend dry ingredients together. Add half of flour mixture to butter mixture then add half of milk. Add in remaining flour mixture then remaining milk.

4. Fill muffin cups almost full. Bake about 15 to 18 minutes or until middle springs back when pressed with finger.

COOKING CLASS

1. A few children can add the topping ingredients together in a 1 cup measure or small bowl.

2. Each child can poke the top of a muffin many times with toothpick or fork. The children can take turns pouring lemonade syrup over muffins using a teaspoon until it all soaks in.

Makes 10 regular sized muffins.
Per muffin: 165 calories, 3.5 g protein, 30 g carbohydrate, 4 g fat, .6 g fiber, 30 mg cholesterol, 270 mg sodium. Calories from fat: 22 percent.

APPLE PIE MUFFINS

INGREDIENTS

nonstick cooking spray
1 large apple (or 2 small)
2 tablespoons sugar
3/4 teaspoon apple pie spice
1 3/4 cups all-purpose flour
1/4 cup sugar
2 teaspoons baking powder

1/4 teaspoon salt
1/4 cup egg substitute
3/4 cup low-fat milk
2 tablespoons canola oil
2 tablespoons applesauce
  or apple butter

TEACHER PREP

1. Preheat oven to 400 degrees.

2. Core and slice apple, then chop into small pieces. (If there's time, this step can be done by the older children using plastic knives.)

3. Coat mini or regular muffin pans with cooking spray or line regular sized muffin pans with paper or foil cups.

COOKING CLASS

1. In medium bowl, measure and blend sugar with apple pie spice. Stir in apple pieces; set aside.

2. In mixing bowl, measure and combine flour, sugar, baking powder, and salt. Make a well in the center.

3. Measure and combine egg substitute, milk, oil, and applesauce; add all at once to flour mixture. Stir just till moistened.

4. Stir in apple mixture. Fill muffin cups 2/3 full.

5. Bake about 20 minutes for regular sized muffins or 12 to 15 minutes for mini muffins (or till golden).

Makes 10 to 12 muffins (or 28 mini muffins).
Per muffin: (if 12 muffins): 136 calories, 3 g protein, 25 g carbohydrate, 2.8 g fat, 1 g fiber, 1 mg cholesterol, 142 mg sodium. Calories from fat: 19 percent.

ORANGE-CRANBERRY MUFFINS

INGREDIENTS

1/2 cup dried cranberries
1/2 cup sugar
2 teaspoons orange zest (grated orange peel), finely chopped
1 3/4 cups flour
2 1/2 teaspoons baking powder
3/4 teaspoon salt

1/4 cup egg substitute
1/3 cup orange juice
1/2 cup low-fat buttermilk
2 tablespoons canola oil
1/4 cup fat-free sour cream
1/2 teaspoon orange extract (optional)

TEACHER PREP

1. Preheat oven to 400 degrees.

2. Coat muffin pan with cooking spray or line with foil or paper muffin cups.

COOKING CLASS

1. Mix cranberries, sugar, and orange zest; set aside.

2. Measure and blend flour, baking powder, and salt in large bowl.

3. In separate bowl combine egg substitute, orange juice, buttermilk, oil, sour cream, and orange extract. Add to dry ingredients, and stir just until moistened.

4. Fold in cranberry mixture.

5. Fill muffin cups 2/3 full. Bake for about 20 minutes or until lightly browned.

Makes 12 muffins.
Per muffin: 216 calories, 3.5 g fiber, 20 mg cholesterol, 182 mg sodium. % Calories from: Protein 9 percent (5 g), Carbohydrate 76 percent (41 g), Fat 15 percent (3.6 g)

CHOCOLATE CHIP MUFFINS

INGREDIENTS

nonstick cooking spray
1/4 cup egg substitute
1/2 cup low-fat milk
1 tablespoon canola oil
3 tablespoons light corn syrup
1 teaspoon vanilla extract

1 1/2 cups flour
1/3 cup sugar
2 teaspoons baking powder
1/2 teaspoon salt
1/2 cup chocolate chips (milk chocolate or semi-sweet)

TEACHER PREP

1. Preheat oven to 400 degrees.

2. Coat 12 muffin cups with cooking spray or line with foil or paper cups.

COOKING CLASS

1. In medium bowl, beat egg substitute with milk, oil, corn syrup, and vanilla.

2. In 4-cup measure or another bowl, stir together flour, sugar, baking powder, and salt; add all at once to egg mixture. Stir just until moistened.

3. Stir in chocolate chips.

4. Fill muffin cups 2/3 full with batter. Bake about 20 minutes or until lightly browned.

Makes 12 muffins.
Per muffin: 144 calories, 3 g protein, 26.5 g carbohydrate, 3.5 g fat, 1 g fiber, 1 mg cholesterol, 191 mg sodium. Calories from fat: 22 percent.

FINDING GOD'S PEACE

The dove has become a common Christian symbol—it's a symbol of God's peace You may see the dove symbol on the back of someone's car. The word *peace* is found throughout the Bible, both in the Old and New testaments, as you'll see in the examples below.

ROMANS 5:1
Therefore, since we have been justified through faith, we have peace with God through our Lord Jesus Christ, through whom we have gained access by faith into this grace in which we now stand.

GALATIANS 5:22-23
But the fruit of the Spirit is love, joy, peace, patience, kindness, goodness, faithfulness, gentleness and self-control.

1 PETER 3:10-12
Whoever would love life and see good days must keep his tongue from evil and his lips from deceitful speech. He must turn from evil and do good; he must seek peace and pursue it. For the eyes of the Lord are on the righteous and his ears are attentive to their prayer, but the face of the Lord is against those who do evil.

BREAD DOVES

EQUIPMENT

large bowl

wooden spoon

measuring cups

9 x 13-inch pan or similar

fork

INGREDIENTS

1 box Pillsbury Hot Roll Mix

1 cup hot water (120-130 degrees F, very hot to the touch)

1 1/2 tablespoons melted margarine or butter

1/4 cup egg substitute

flour

nonstick cooking spray

7 whole almonds

14 dried cranberries or raisins

TEACHER PREP

1. Combine contents of box and yeast packet from box in large bowl; mix well. Stir in hot water, melted butter and egg substitute. Continue to stir until dough pulls away from sides of bowl.

2. Knead dough on floured surface for about 5 minutes or until smooth.

3. Cover dough with large bowl; let rest 5 minutes.

4. Divide dough evenly into 8 pieces.

5. Coat a 9 x 13-inch pan with cooking spray.

6. Preheat oven to 375 degrees.

COOKING CLASS

1. Hand 7 children a piece of dough (leave the 8th piece for the heads). Show for the children how to shape the dough into a dove's body and tail. Use a fork to mark the tail feathers.

2. Divide the last piece of dough into 7 small pieces. Have each child roll their piece into a ball and set on their dove body for a head.

3. Show the children how to stick the almond (for the beak) and cranberries (for the eyes) into the dove's head. When done, the children can place doves into prepared pan.

4. Cover and let rise in warm place (on top of preheating oven will do nicely) for 20 minutes.

5. The teacher can now uncover rolls and bake for 15 to 20 minutes or until golden brown. Brush doves with melted butter if desired.

Makes about 7 bread doves.
Per dove: 246 calories, 7 g protein, 42 g carbohydrate, 4.5 g fat, 7 mg cholesterol, 439 mg sodium, 1 g fiber. Calories from fat: 17 percent.

REACHING THE PROMISED LAND

Manna is the special food God gave daily to the Israelites until they reached the promised land. It was an example of how God watched over his people and provided what they needed.

EXODUS 16:31
The people of Israel called the bread manna. It was white like coriander seed and tasted like wafers made with honey.

EXODUS 16:35
The Israelites ate manna forty years, until they came to a land that was settled; they ate manna until they reached the border of Canaan.

MANNA PASTRY

EQUIPMENT

9 x 13-inch baking pan
measuring cup
spoon

zester tool (for orange)
small bowl

INGREDIENTS

nonstick cooking spray
8-ounce can reduced-fat refrigerated
  crescent dinner rolls

1/4 cup honey
1 orange
1/2 cup chopped walnuts or pecans

TEACHER PREP

1. Preheat oven to 375 degrees.

2. Coat 9 x 13-inch baking pan with cooking spray.

COOKING CLASS

1. Have one of the children open the can of crescent roll dough. Then have one or two children roll the dough out in the prepared pan to cover the bottom (it should fit well).

2. One child can drizzle the honey evenly over the dough. Spread the honey evenly with a spoon if necessary.

3. Another child can use a zesting tool (a grater can also be used if a zester is not available) to remove much of the orange zest (peel) from the orange. An adult should finely chop these small strands of orange peel.

4. In a small bowl, toss the orange zest with the chopped nuts. (A child can use a hand grinder or chopper if the nuts need to chopped.) Sprinkle the nut mixture evenly over the dough.

5. Bake the dough for 10 to 12 minutes or until lightly browned. Cut the rectangle in half vertically and horizontally then cut each square diagonally twice to make 4 triangles in each square (16 triangles altogether).

Per serving: 90 calories, 2 g protein, 11 g carbohydrate, 4.3 g fat, 0 mg cholesterol, 1 g fiber, 115 mg sodium. Calories from fat: 43 percent.

CELEBRATING OUR INDIVIDUALITY

When God created us, he made us each unique—like every snowflake is unique. God knows and loves us completely. God knows the number of hairs on our head. We are all different, right down to our thumbprint.

MATTHEW 10:30
And even the very hairs of your head are all numbered.

THUMBPRINT COOKIE DOUGH

INGREDIENTS

1/4 cup fat-free cream cheese
7 tablespoons butter or margarine, softened
1 1/2 cups all-purpose flour
1/2 cup sugar
1/4 cup egg substitute

1 1/2 teaspoons vanilla extract
1/2 teaspoon almond or lemon extract
2/3 cup finely chopped walnuts or pecans
1/2 cup reduced-sugar jam or preserves

In mixing bowl beat cream cheese with butter until well blended. Add half the flour to the butter mixture. Then add the sugar, egg substitute, and vanilla and almond extracts. Beat until thoroughly blended. Beat in remaining flour. Cover and chill in refrigerator about 2 hours or overnight.

JAM THUMBPRINT COOKIES

EQUIPMENT

cookie sheets

nonstick cooking spray

several shallow bowls

several teaspoons

TEACHER PREP

1. Make thumbprint dough the day before needed by following the recipe directions on the previous page. You may need to double the recipe.

2. Before cooking class, preheat oven to 375 degrees.

3. Coat cookie sheets with cooking spray.

4. Set chopped nuts in several shallow bowls. Set several jars of jam or preserves out with teaspoons.

COOKING CLASS

1. Show the children how to make 1-inch balls with the dough. The children can then roll each ball in the nuts, then place them on the cookie sheet.

2. Demonstrate how to make an indentation in the center of the cookie using your thumb. After the children have put a thumbprint in each cookie, they can fill the centers with about 1/2 to 3/4 teaspoon jam or preserves.

3. The teacher can now bake the cookies (they take about 8 to 10 minutes to bake) while the children go on to Sunday school. When Sunday school is finished, they will not only have a tasty treat waiting for them, but some of the cookies can be served to others.

Makes 2 to 3 dozen cookies, depending on the size of the balls.

Per cookie: (if 3 dozen per batch): 76 calories, 1.5 g protein, 9 g carbohydrate, 3.5 g fat, .5 g fiber, 6 mg cholesterol, 38 mg sodium. Calories from fat: 45 percent.

REMEMBERING GOD'S LAWS

This a great way to reinforce and memorize the Ten Commandments while making a cake.

1 JOHN 3:24
Those who obey his commandments live in him, and he in them.

CAKE INGREDIENTS
THE 10 COMMANDMENTS

1. LEAVENER (baking powder,baking soda) **L**ove the Lord your God with all your heart and with all your soul and with all your mind.

2. NUTS Love your **N**eighbor as yourself.

3. FLOUR Thou shalt not worship **F**alse idols.

4. VANILLA & ORANGE EXTRACTS Thou shalt not take the Lord's name in **V**ain.

5. SALT & SPICES Remember the **S**abbath day by keeping it holy.

6. PANCAKE SYRUP Honor your **P**arents.

7. MARGARINE OR BUTTER Thou shalt not **M**urder

8. CRACKER CRUMBS Thou shalt not **C**ommit adultery.

9. SWEETENERS (SUGAR AND ORANGE JUICE) Thou shalt not **S**teal.

10. TOPPING Thou shalt not give false **T**estimony against your neighbor.

Note: the only cake ingredient not included in this list is eggs.

TEN COMMANDMENT CAKE

EQUIPMENT

10-inch tube pan
measuring cups
measuring spoons
electric mixer

spatula
small cup or 2-cup measure
spoon

INGREDIENTS

1 cup graham cracker crumbs
2/3 cup sugar
2/3 cup light pancake syrup
1 teaspoon baking powder
1 teaspoon baking soda
1 teaspoon salt
1 1/2 teaspoons pumpkin pie spice
1/3 cup margarine, butter,
  or shortening

1 cup orange juice
1/2 teaspoon vanilla extract
1/2 teaspoon orange extract
2 cups flour
1 egg and 1/3 cup egg substitute
1/2 cup chopped nuts (pecans or
  walnuts work well)

TOPPING

1 cup powdered sugar

2 tablespoons orange juice

TEACHER PREP

1. Set out all the cake ingredients and equipment.

2. Spray 10-inch tube pan with cooking spray.

3. Preheat oven to 350 degrees.

COOKING CLASS

1. Assign one student to each ingredient. Each student (not including the students assigned to nuts and topping) can recite the commandment that corresponds to their assigned ingredient as they add the ingredient to a large bowl.

2. One of the children can add the egg and egg substitute to the mixing bowl now.

3. The teacher can now mix the cake ingredients with an electric mixer on low speed to blend. Scrape sides of bowl with spatula. Then beat the mixture on medium speed for about 3 minutes.

4. Now the student who was assigned nuts can stir them into the cake batter.

5. The teacher can spoon the batter into prepared tube pan. Bake for 40 to 45 minutes or until cake tester comes out clean.

6. While the cake is baking, the student assigned topping can now blend the topping ingredients in a small bowl or 2 cup measure with a spoon. Set aside. Let cake cool for about 15 minutes in the plan, then invert onto serving plate. Drizzle the topping over the top.

Makes 16 servings.
Per serving: 240 calories, 3.5 g protein, 39.5 g carbohydrate, 8 g fat, 13 mg cholesterol, 335 mg sodium, 1 g fiber. Calories from fat: 30 percent.

OPTION: Use 2 round cake pans instead of a 10-inch tube pan. It will take about 25 to 30 minutes to bake (instead of 40 to 45 minutes). Double the topping recipe and there will be enough for both cakes. If making this cake at home, you will now have one cake to keep and one to give to a friend, family member, or neighbor.

LINKING TO THE PAST

Several foods, such as leeks and onions, are mentioned in stories of the Old Testament. Eating a soup that contains foods mentioned in the Old Testament is one way of remembering the wealth of important messages and stories found in the Bible.

NUMBERS 11: 4-5
The rabble with them began to crave other food, and again the Israelites started wailing and said, "If only we had meat to eat! We remember the fish we ate in Egypt at no cost—also the cucumbers, melons, leeks, onions and garlic."

CREAM OF OLD TESTAMENT SOUP

EQUIPMENT

fork	potato masher
grater	large, nonstick saucepan
plastic knife	measuring cup

INGREDIENTS

6 green onions, chopped	4 potatoes
2 leeks	1 1/4 cups whole milk
1 tablespoon butter or margarine	1 cup (firmly packed) grated reduced-fat sharp cheddar cheese
1 teaspoon garlic powder or 2 small cloves garlic, minced or pressed	pepper to taste
2 cups low-sodium chicken broth	

TEACHER PREP
1. Cut off the very tops of the leeks, wash well, and thinly slice.

----

2. Pierce potatoes with fork several times and microwave on high until tender. Let cool.

3. Grate cheddar cheese if needed, or have an older child do it during cooking class.

COOKING CLASS

1. A couple of children can peel the potatoes and mash with a potato masher.

2. A couple of children can chop the green onions using a plastic knife.

3. An adult should melt butter in a large nonstick saucepan over medium heat. Add leeks and green onions and sauté for about four minutes.

4. A child can add 1/4 cup of the broth, another can measure and add the garlic powder, and another can add the mashed potatoes while the adult stirs.

5. Gradually stir in the remaining milk and broth. Continue to cook, stirring, for a few more minutes.

6. A child can add the grated cheese while an adult stirs until it melts.

Makes 5 servings.
Per serving: 280 calories, 13 g protein, 38 g carbohydrate, 9 g fat, 3.5 g fiber, 27 mg cholesterol, 212 mg sodium. Calories from fat: 28 percent.

REMEMBERING IMPORTANT MESSAGES

Several foods are mentioned in stories in the New Testament. Jesus fed 5,000, for example, with loaves of bread and fish. When John was baptizing in the desert region, he ate locusts and wild honey. Eating tuna melt sandwiches on honey-wheat bread is one way to remember the important messages and stories in the New Testament.

MARK 1:6

John wore clothing made of camel's hair, with a leather belt around his waist, and he ate locusts and wild honey.

TUNA MELT

EQUIPMENT

bread machine
can opener

medium bowl

INGREDIENTS

1/2 loaf Honey-Walnut Wheat
  Bread (see recipe below)
12-ounce can water-packed solid
  white tuna, drained
1/4 cup low-fat mayonnaise
1 large stalk celery or 2 small stalks,
  finely chopped

pepper to taste
3 green onions, chopped (optional)
6 ounces reduced-fat sharp cheddar
  cheese, grated

TEACHER PREP

1. The night before needed, prepare honey-walnut wheat bread using a 1 1/2 pound or 2 pound bread machine and the recipe below.

2. The day needed, slice bread into about 12 large slices per loaf.

COOKING CLASS

1. Children can add drained tuna, celery, mayonnaise, pepper, and onions if desired, to bowl. Blend well.

2. Six children can spread 1/4 cup of tuna mixture over a slice of bread. (Save the rest of the loaf for another use.) Have each child sprinkle 1/4 cup of grated cheese over the top.

3. Broil the open-face sandwich until cheese is melted.

Makes about 6 open-faced sandwiches.
Per open-faced sandwich: 332 calories, 27 g protein, 32 g carbohydrate, 10.5 g fat, 2 g fiber, 37 mg cholesterol, 588 mg sodium. Calories from fat: 29 percent.

HONEY-WALNUT WHEAT BREAD
(for 1 1/2 pound or 2 pound bread machine)

INGREDIENTS

1 cup plus 2 tablespoons water
1/4 cup honey
1 tablespoon butter or margarine, softened
2 cups bread flour

1 cup whole wheat flour
1/3 cup chopped walnuts
1 teaspoon salt
1 1/2 teaspoon bread machine yeast

PREPARATION

Measure each ingredient carefully, placing all ingredients in bread machine pan in the order recommended by the manufacturer. Select the basic/white setting. Use medium or light crust color. (It should take about 4 hours from start to finish.) Remove baked bread from pan and cool on wire rack.

Makes 12 slices.
Per slice: 162 calories, 4.5 g protein, 29.5 g carbohydrate, 3 g fat, 3 mg cholesterol, 2 g fiber, 190 mg sodium. Calories from fat: 18 percent.

HELPING SOMEONE IN NEED

Jesus fed 5,000 hungry people once. You might be able to help feed a family in need—someone may need help in your very own neighborhood or in your very own church. Below you will find a few quick recipes you can make to feed a family.

MARK 6:30-44

The apostles gathered around Jesus and reported to him all they had done and taught. Then, because so many people were coming and going that they did not even have a chance to eat, he said to them, "Come with me by yourselves to a quiet place and get some rest."

So they went away by themselves in a boat to a solitary place. But many who saw them leaving recognized them and ran on foot from all the towns and got there ahead of them. When Jesus landed and saw a large crowd, he had compassion on them, because they were like sheep without a shepherd. So he began teaching them many things.

By this time it was late in the day, so his disciples came to him. "This is a remote place," they said, "and it's already very late. Send the people away so they can go to the surrounding countryside and villages and buy themselves something to eat."

But he answered, "You give them something to eat."

They said to him, "That would take eight months of a man's wages! Are we to go and spend that much on bread and give it to them to eat?"

"How many loaves do you have?" he asked. "Go and see."

When they found out, they said, "Five—and two fish."

Then Jesus directed them to have all the people sit down in groups on the green grass. So they sat down in groups of hundreds and fifties. Taking the five loaves and the two fish and looking up to heaven, he gave thanks and broke the loaves. Then he gave them to his disciples to set before the people. He also divided the two fish among them all. They all ate and were satisfied, and the disciples picked up twelve basketfuls of broken pieces of bread and fish. The number of the men who had eaten was five thousand.

1-2-3-LASAGNA

EQUIPMENT

9 x 13-inch baking pan
non-stick frypan
measuring cups
knife

2 medium-size bowls or 4-cup measures
foil
cheese grater

INGREDIENTS

1 pound ground sirloin or super lean ground beef (9% fat)
1 cup water
2 cups bottled spaghetti sauce (with 1 gram fat per 1/2 cup)
1 cup bottled spaghetti sauce
1 cup water
15 ounces part-skim ricotta cheese (low-fat can also be used)
1/3 cup grated Parmesan cheese

black pepper to taste (about 1/2 teaspoon)
1 teaspoon Italian Herb Seasoning or Fines Herbs
4-6 green onions, chopped
1/4 cup egg substitute
12 extra wide lasagna noodles (336 g)
3/4 cup grated mozzarella cheese
3/4 cup grated reduced fat sharp cheddar cheese

TEACHER PREP

1. Preheat oven to 375 degrees. Set out a 9 x 13-inch baking pan or dish.

2. Brown ground beef in a non-stick frypan. Stir in 1 cup water and 2 cups spaghetti sauce; set aside.

3. Wash, trim, and chop green onions.

COOKING CLASS

1. One child can blend 1 cup of spaghetti sauce with 1 cup water in a medium bowl or 4 cup measure; set aside.

2. Several children can measure and blend ricotta cheese, Parmesan cheese, black pepper, herbs, green onions, and egg substitute in another bowl or 4 cup measure.

3. The children can help assemble the lasagna:

> ➡Spread 1 1/2 cups of spaghetti sauce mixture in bottom of pan.

> ➡Top with 3 (uncooked) lasagna noodles.

> ➡Spread 1 1/2 cups of beef mixture evenly over the noodles.

> ➡Top with 3 more noodles.

> ➡Spread half of ricotta cheese mixture over the noodles.

> ➡Top with 3 more noodles.

> ➡Spread 1 1/2 cups of beef mixture over noodles.

> ➡Top with 3 more noodles.

> ➡Spread remaining ricotta cheese mixture over noodles. Spread any remaining meat sauce and other remaining spaghetti sauce (about 1/2 cup) over the cheese mixture.

4. An adult can cover pan tightly with foil and bake for 1 hour.

5. While lasagna is baking, someone can grate the mozzarella and cheddar cheeses if needed.

6. Remove foil and sprinkle grated cheeses over the lasagna. Bake 5 minutes or until cheese is melted.

Makes 12 servings.
Per serving: 297 calories, 22 g protein, 28 g carbohydrate, 10.4 g fat, 35 mg cholesterol, 2 g fiber, 453 mg sodium. Calories from fat: 31 percent.

GARLIC CHEESE TOAST

EQUIPMENT

garlic press
small food processor or electric
  mixer

serrated knife
measuring cups
spoon

INGREDIENTS

4 tablespoons butter, softened
1/4 cup fat-free cream cheese
1/4 cup grated Parmesan cheese

1 garlic clove
1 loaf sourdough or French bread
  (16 ounces)

TEACHER PREP

1. Set oven to broil.

2. Set out garlic press and small food processor or electric mixer.

3. Use a serrated knife to cut loaf horizontally into two halves.

COOKING CLASS

1. Children can measure butter, cream cheese, and Parmesan cheese, and place in food processor or mixing bowl.

2. One child can peel skin off garlic clove and add to garlic press. Press garlic, and add garlic to butter mixture.

3. Blend until smooth; spread mixture evenly on both bread halves with spoon.

4. An adult can now broil the bread halves briefly until lightly browned.

Makes 10 servings.
Per serving: 183 calories, 6 g protein, 24 g carbohydrate, 6.5 g fat, 15 mg cholesterol, 1.5 g fiber, 400 mg sodium. Calories from fat: 33 percent.

CRUSTLESS VEGETABLE QUICHE

EQUIPMENT

10-inch pie plate
large nonstick frypan
plastic knives
garlic press
cheese grater

measuring teaspoons
4 cup measure
electric mixer and mixing bowl
spatula

INGREDIENTS

nonstick cooking spray
2 stalks broccoli
8 mushrooms
2 cloves garlic
3/4 cup chopped onion
3/4 teaspoon oregano flakes
3/4 teaspoon basil flakes

6 eggs
1 1/2 cups egg substitute
approximately 1/2 cup low-fat milk
4 ounces reduced-fat sharp
   cheddar cheese
4 ounces reduced-fat Jack or
   Swiss cheese

TEACHER PREP

1. Preheat oven to 350 degrees.

COOKING CLASS

1. One of the children can coat the pie plate with cooking spray.

2. Put several children to work preparing the vegetables: someone can wash and chop the broccoli into bite-size pieces with a plastic knife; someone can wash and slice the mushrooms with a plastic knife; and someone can peel the garlic then use a garlic press to crush it; and someone can chop the onion with a plastic knife if it hasn't already been done.

3. One of the children can grate the cheese using a cheese grater.

4. One of the children coat the frypan with cooking spray. An adult can help the child saute broccoli, mushrooms, onions, and garlic. A little broth or water can be added if moisture is needed during cooking.

5. Another child can measure and add oregano and basil to frypan. Cook the mixture until vegetables are just tender.

6. An older child or an adult can crack the eggs and add them to a 4 cup measure. Someone else can measure the egg substitute and add it

to the eggs. Add milk until mixture equals 3 1/2 cups. Someone can pour the egg mixture into mixing bowl and beat until blended.

7. Have one of the children spread half of the grated cheese in the bottom of pie plate. Add the vegetable mixture. Another child can top the vegetables with the rest of the cheese. Pour egg mixture gently over the cheese and vegetables and bake for 40 minutes or until set.

Makes 8 servings.
Per serving: 180 calories, 19 g protein, 5 g carbohydrate, 9 g fat, 2 g fiber, 174 mg cholesterol, 295 mg sodium. Calories from fat: 45 percent.

THIRST QUENCHERS

People need food and drink to survive. Many times God and Jesus provided drink for their thirsty followers. Many times God and Jesus performed miracles in order to do this.

EXODUS 15:22-25

Then Moses led Israel from the Red Sea and they went into the Desert of Shur. For three days they traveled in the desert without finding water. When they came to Marah, they could not drink its water because it was bitter. (That is why the place is called Marah.) So the people grumbled against Moses, saying, "What are we to drink?"

Then Moses cried out to the Lord, and the Lord showed him a piece of wood. He threw it into the water, and the water became sweet.

JOHN 2:7-11

Jesus said to the servants, "Fill the jars with water;" so they filled them to the brim. Then he told them, "Now draw some out and take it to the master of the banquet."

They did so, and the master of the banquet tasted the water that had been turned into wine. He did not realize where it had come from, though the servants who had drawn the water knew. Then he called the bridegroom aside and said, "Everyone brings out the choice wine first and then the cheaper wine after the guests have had too much to drink; but you have saved the best till now."

This, the first of his miraculous signs, Jesus performed in Cana of Galilee. He thus revealed his glory, and his disciples put their faith in him.

FRUIT JUICE PUNCH

EQUIPMENT

punch bowl and punch bowl ladle   serving cups
4 cup measure

INGREDIENTS

4 cups bottled cherry juice
4 cups orange juice (pulp free
   if possible)
4 cups apple juice

4 cups diet Sprite, diet 7up, or
   diet ginger ale
ice cubes (optional)

TEACHER PREP

1. Set out punch bowl and ladle.

2. Set out cups.

COOKING CLASS

1. Have different children measure 4 cups of each ingredient and pour it into the punch bowl.

2. One of the children can stir the punch while the ingredients are being added.

3. Ice cubes can be added by another child.

4. The children can use the ladle to fill cups with punch. The punch can be served after church.

Makes 16 (8 ounce) servings.
Per cup of punch: 93 calories, .5 g protein, 23 g carbohydrates, 0 fat, 0 cholesterol, 6 mg sodium. Calories from fat: 0.

HOMEMADE LEMONADE

EQUIPMENT

several citrus juicers (if possible)

several 2 cup measures
  or small bowls

slotted spoon (if you don't have a
  juicer that strains out seeds)

2/3 cup measuring cup

2 quart pitchers

INGREDIENTS

about 5 lemons (to make 1 cup
  of lemon juice)

4 cups water

2/3 cup sugar

ice cubes (optional)

TEACHER PREP

1. Wash lemons and cut each lemon in half crosswise.

COOKING CLASS

1. Show the children how to hold a citrus juicer atop a 2 cup measure or small bowl, and press each half of lemon into the citrus juicer, turning the lemon left and right until most of the juice is pushed out. Have enough lemon halves for each child to try it.

2. The children can throw away any pulp or seeds that have collected in the juice. (If you aren't using this type of juicer, use a slotted spoon to fish the seeds out.)

3. Once the class has collected 1 cup of lemon juice, they can pour it in the pitcher.

4. One of the children can measure 4 cups of water and add it to the pitcher. Someone else can measure 2/3 cup sugar and add it to the pitcher.

5. A child can now stir the mixture until the sugar dissolves. Add ice now if desired.

Makes 5 (8 ounce) servings.
Per serving: 116 calories, 0 protein 31 g carbohydrate, 0 fat, .2 g fiber, 0 cholesterol, 1 mg sodium. Calories from fat: 0.

THE SECRET FISH SYMBOL

A long time ago when Christians were being persecuted, they used a secret symbol so they would know whether they were among other Christians and could worship the Lord in safety. Often they drew this symbol in the sand. The symbol they used was the fish. Perhaps you've seen the fish symbol on cars driven by Christians.

Fish was often associated with Jesus in the Bible and in the life of the early church. The fish symbol has come to mean Jesus and the Christian tradition. Drawing the fish symbol was often how groups of Christians found one another during the times of the early church.

SWEET FISH PRETZELS

EQUIPMENT

2 pound loaf bread machine
  (if using bread machine)
mixer and large mixing bowl
  (if not using bread machine)

measuring cups and measuring spoons
zesting tool
2 large cookie sheets

INGREDIENTS

1 cup low-fat milk
3 tablespoons light corn syrup
  or honey
1 egg
1/4 cup egg substitute
2 1/2 tablespoons margarine or
  butter (melted, if using bread
  machine)

zest (finely grated peel) from
  2 lemons
4 1/3 cups bread flour or all-purpose
  flour
1/4 cup sugar
1/2 teaspoon salt
3 teaspoons bread machine yeast
  or active dry yeast

OPTIONAL TOPPINGS

melted butter or margarine
cinnamon-sugar mixture (1/2 teaspoon ground cinnamon to 1 tablespoon
  sugar)
Vanilla or Lemon Glaze (1 cup powdered sugar, 1/2 teaspoon vanilla or lemon
  extract, 1 tablespoon milk plus a teaspoon or two more if needed)

TEACHER PREP WITH BREAD MACHINE

1. Two hours before dough is needed, place all ingredients in the
bread machine in the order recommended by the manufacturer. Set
machine to "dough" setting (this will mix the dough and allow it to
rise once).

TEACHER PREP WITHOUT BREAD MACHINE

1. About 2 hours before needed, in large mixing bowl, combine 1 1/2
cups of the flour and the yeast; set aside. In saucepan heat the milk,
corn syrup, margarine, sugar, and salt just till warm (120 to 130
degrees) and margarine almost melts.

2. Add milk mixture to flour mixture in mixing bowl. Add egg and
egg substitute. Beat with mixer on low to medium for 30 seconds.
Scrape sides of bowl and beat on high speed for 3 minutes. Stir in as
much remaining flour as you can.

3. On floured surface, knead in enough of remaining flour to make a soft dough that is smooth and elastic (about 4 minutes). Shape into a ball. Place in a greased bowl; turn once. Cover and let rise in warm place till double (about 1 hour).

4. Punch down dough. Cut dough into 4 quarters. Divide each quarter into 4 or 5 pieces (to make 16 to 20 pretzels).

5. Prepare a floured surface in the kitchen for the children.

6. Fifteen minutes before cooking class, preheat oven to 375 degrees.

7. Prepare optional toppings if you choose to use them. Mix up the glaze or cinnamon-sugar mixture, or melt the butter.

COOKING CLASS

1. Give each child a piece of dough and show them how to make a rope by rolling the dough on the floured surface with their hands.

2. Now show the children how to shape their rope into a fish symbol.

3. Set the pretzel fish on cookie sheets, and place on top of warmed oven to rest for 10 minutes.

4. Bake for about 15 minutes or until lightly browned.

5. Children can dip top of pretzel fish in melted butter then sprinkle with cinnamon-sugar mixture if desired. Or, children can spread vanilla or lemon glaze over the top of their pretzel fish if desired.

Makes about 20 pretzel fish.
Per pretzel: 140 calories, 4 g protein, 26 g carbohydrate, 2 g fat, 1 g fiber, 15 mg cholesterol, 86 mg sodium. Calories from fat: 14 percent.

REMEMBERING THE BIRTH OF MOSES

Moses was one of the most important people in the Old Testament. He led the Israelites out of Egypt and continued to lead them many years after. The scripture below tells of his birth and how he was saved so he could later lead his people.

EXODUS 2:1-10

Now a man of the house of Levi married a Levite woman, and she became pregnant and gave birth to a son. When she saw that he was a fine child, she hid him for three months. But when she could hide him no longer, she got a papyrus basket for him and coated it with tar and pitch. Then she placed the child in it and put it among the reeds along the bank of the Nile. His sister stood at a distance to see what would happen to him.

Then Pharaoh's daughter went down to the Nile to bathe, and her attendants were walking along the river bank. She saw the basket among the reeds and sent her slave girl to get it. She opened it and saw the baby. He was crying and she felt sorry for him. "This is one of the Hebrew babies," she said.

Then his sister asked Pharaoh's daughter, "Shall I go and get one of the Hebrew women to nurse the baby for you?"

"Yes, go," she answered. And the girl went and got the baby's mother. Pharaoh's daughter said to her, "Take this baby and nurse him for me, and I will pay you." So the woman took the baby and nursed him. When the child grew older, she took him to Pharaoh's daughter and he became her son. She named him Moses, saying, "I drew him out of the water."

- - - -

MINI MOSES ROOT BEER FLOATS

EQUIPMENT

plastic cups
1/2 cup measuring cup

2-inch wide cookie scoop or
  mini ice-cream scoop
plastic spoons

INGREDIENTS (PER ICE CREAM FLOAT)

1/2 cup diet root beer
  (regular can also be used)
1 cookie scoop of light vanilla ice
  cream or light vanilla frozen
  yogurt (1/4 cup)

1 reduced-fat Nilla Wafer
  (or other wafer cookie)

TEACHER PREP

1. Set out equipment and ingredients.

COOKING CLASS

1. Show the children how to make a Root Beer Float:

➡Pour about 1/2 cup of root beer in your cup.

➡Add a scoop ice cream.

2. Place a Nilla Wafer in the ice cream.

Per Root Beer Float: 65 calories, 2 g protein, 10 g carbohydrate, 2.2 g fat, 12 mg cholesterol, 30 mg sodium. Calories from fat: 30 percent.

WATCHING GOD'S LOVE GROW

In this modern day and age, it is so easy for adults and children to get caught up in trying to become rich, thin, or beautiful. But the true meaning of life and happiness has nothing to do being rich or beautiful.

The meaning of life is to grow in our faith toward God, to become better, wiser people, and to love others and to be loved. We cannot truly find happiness in life without these things. All these things come from love. And all love comes from God.

And the wonderful thing about love is that it never stops growing. Because God loves us, we can love ourselves and love others. And because we love others, they are more likely to love themselves and to love others.

1 JOHN 4:7-8
Dear friends, let us love one another, for love comes from God.
Everyone who love has been born of God and knows God.
Whoever does not love does not know God, because God is love.

1 JOHN 4:16
And so we know and rely on the love God has for us.
God is love. Whoever lives in love lives in God, and God in him.

OVERNIGHT CINNAMON ROLLS

EQUIPMENT

2 pound bread machine
measuring cups
measuring spoons
2 9-inch round or square pans

2 small bowls
rolling pin
serrated knife

INGREDIENTS

1 1/4 cups + 3 tablespoons water
3 tablespoons diet margarine
3 3/4 cups bread flour

6 tablespoons sugar
1 1/2 teaspoons salt
2 teaspoons bread machine yeast

CINNAMON FILLING

1/2 cup sugar
3 teaspoons ground cinnamon

3 tablespoons diet margarine

VANILLA GLAZE

1 cup powdered sugar
1/2 teaspoon vanilla

1 1/2 tablespoons milk

COOKING CLASS

1. Measure bread ingredients carefully, placing all of them in the bread machine pan in the order recommended by the manufacturer. (Usually you are told to add the water and margarine first, then add the flour and sugar. Place the salt in one of the corners of the pan and make a well in the center of the flour for the yeast.)

2. Select the dough cycle on your bread machine (this cycle should take about 1 hour and 40 minutes). Meanwhile, coat two 9-inch round or square pans with nonstick cooking spray. Blend the sugar and cinnamon for the filling in a small bowl.

3. When the dough cycle is complete, flatten the dough with floured hands or rolling pin into a 9 x 13-inch rectangle on a lightly floured surface. Spread with 3 tablespoons diet margarine; sprinkle with cinnamon-sugar mixture. Roll dough up tightly from the 13-inch side. Seal the seam of the dough by pinching it into the roll. An adult can cut the roll into 1-inch slices with a serrated knife. Place 6 or 7 rolls in

each pan. Cover and place in the refrigerator overnight. In the morning the rolls should be double in size.

4. Preheat oven to 375 degrees. Bake about 25 minutes or until
golden brown. While rolls are baking, mix all glaze ingredients in a
small bowl until smooth. Drizzle vanilla glaze over the warm rolls.

Makes about 13 rolls.
Per roll: 228 calories, 4 g protein, 46 g carbohydrate, 3 g fat, .2 mg cholesterol,
271 mg sodium. Calories from fat: 12 percent.

OBSERVING GOOD FRIDAY

During the reign of Elizabeth I, sweetened and spiced breads were only allowed to be made on special occasions. Good Friday was one of the occasions and hot cross buns were one of the popular sweetened breads. Since that time, hot cross buns have been associated with Good Friday. It was believed that if the buns were actually made on Good Friday, they would protect the baker, and those sharing them, from misfortune in the coming year.

Making hot cross buns is also a reminder of the cross and what it means to all of us.

HEBREWS 12:2
Let us fix our eyes on Jesus, the author and perfecter of our faith, who for the joy set before him endured the cross, scorning its shame, and sat down at the right hand of the throne of God.

EQUIPMENT

2 pound bread machine (optional) or large mixing bowl	serrated knife
measuring cups	small bowl or 2-cup measure
measuring spoons	2 Tbsp. milk
2 baking sheets	small spoon
	pastry bag or decorator's press

TEACHER PREP

You have a couple of options. You can make the basic sweet dough using the dough setting of your 2 pound bread machine or you can make the dough by hand. You can make the dough in the evening, then after the first rise, shape into buns and place in baking pans. Cover, place the pans in the refrigerator, and let rise a second time overnight. Cook the buns the next morning just in time for the cooking class.

1. Prepare dough according to recipe below using a 2 pound bread machine or by hand. Let rise once in bread machine or in warm place.

2. If you want the optional raisins and chopped cherries, knead these into the dough now. Shape into buns the night before, place in baking pans, cover, and let rise overnight. If preparing the dough the day you need it, shape into buns, place in baking pans, cover, and let rise in a warm place for about an hour.

3. About 15 minutes before you bake the buns, preheat oven to 350 degrees. Just before they go in the oven, gently cut a cross in each bun using a serrated knife.

4. Bake 20 to 25 minutes or until they're golden brown.

5. While the buns are baking, spoon lemon curd into a decorators press or pastry bag using the star tip.

6. If pressed for class time, mix up the glaze ahead of time.

COOKING CLASS

1. If you aren't pressed for time, have a couple of the children make the glaze by blending 1 cup powdered sugar and 1 teaspoon vanilla in a small bowl or 2 cup measure. Gradually have them add 2 tablespoons milk until the consistency is right for drizzling.

2. Have the children spread the glaze over the entire top of the warm buns using a small spoon.

3. The children can now make a cross on the buns using the decorator's press or pastry bag filled with lemon curd. The buns are now ready to be enjoyed.

HOT CROSS BUNS

INGREDIENTS

1/2 cup warm low-fat milk
1 teaspoon sugar
2 tablespoons or packets active
 dry yeast
1/2 cup all-purpose or bread flour
1 cup warm low-fat milk
1/3 cup brown sugar
1 egg
1/4 cup egg substitute
1 cup all-purpose or bread flour
1/4 cup butter, melted

1/4 cup low-fat lemon yogurt
1 1/2 teaspoons salt
2 teaspoons apple pie spice (or use
 1 teaspoon ground cinnamon,
 1/2 teaspoon nutmeg, and
 1/2 teaspoon allspice)
1/2 cup chopped maraschino cherries
 and 1/2 cup raisins (optional)
4 cups all-purpose or bread flour
approximately 1/2 cup lemon curd
 (in jam section of most grocery stores)

GLAZE

1 cup powdered sugar
1 teaspoon vanilla

2 tablespoons low-fat milk

PREPARATION

1. Put 1/2 cup warm milk in large mixing bowl; mix in the sugar, yeast, and 1/2 cup flour. Let sit 10 minutes until bubbly. Add 1 cup warm milk and 1/3 cup brown sugar to the yeast mixture in bowl. Beat in the egg, egg substitute, and 1 cup flour. On low speed, beat in butter, yogurt, salt, spices, and raisins and cherries if desired. Mix in the remaining 4 cups flour until the dough holds together and pulls away from the sides of the bowl.

2. Knead dough on a floured surface for a few minutes. Wash and lightly grease the mixing bowl with butter or shortening. Add dough to bowl, turning once to coat all sides with butter. Cover the bowl and let the dough rise in a warm place for about 1 1/2 hours.

3. Punch it down on floured surface. Divide the dough in half and divide each half into 8 or so pieces. Roll each piece into a ball and place on 2 baking sheets that have been coated with nonstick cooking

spray. Let rise until double, about 45 minutes (or overnight in refrigerator). Preheat oven to 350 degrees. Just before baking, gently cut a cross in each bun using a serrated knife. Bake for about 20 minutes or until golden brown.

4. While baking, put lemon curd in decorator's press or pastry bag using a star tip. Blend glaze ingredients together in small bowl or 2 cup measure, adding enough milk to make it drizzling consistency.

5. Spread the glaze over the entire top of the warm buns using a small spoon. Make a cross on the buns with lemon curd.

Makes about 16 hot cross buns.
Per bun: 235 calories, 6 g protein, 43 g carbohydrate, 4 g fat, 23 mg cholesterol, 280 sodium. Calories from fat: 16 percent.

THE TRUE MEANING OF EASTER

Easter is truly not about chocolate bunnies and jelly beans (although those are certainly things we all enjoy)—it is about the resurrection of Christ. This Jelly Bean Easter Prayer is a way of remembering the awesomeness of God's love and Jesus' life and death and what it means to you and me.

LUKE 24:1-48

(Verses 44-48) He said to them, "This is what I told you while I was still with you: Everything must be fulfilled that is written about me in the Law of Moses, the Prophets and the Psalms."

Then he opened their minds so they could understand the Scriptures. He told them, "This is what is written: The Christ will suffer and rise from the dead on the third day, and repentance and forgiveness of sins will be preached in his name to all nations, beginning at Jerusalem. You are witnesses of these things.

EQUIPMENT

scissors

8 serving bowls

saran wrap or snack-size zip-lock bags

gift ribbon if needed

TEACHER PREP

These Jelly Bean Easter Prayer pouches will help children celebrate and spread the good news that Jesus Christ has risen!

1. Make copies of the Jelly Bean Easter Prayer and cut into small cards (at least two for each child; one to keep and one or more to give away).

2. Buy jelly beans for your class plus plenty of extra. You'll need equal quantities of red, green, yellow, blue, black, white , purple, and pink. Place each color in a different serving bowl. If you can't but the different colors separately, buy jelly beans in bulk, all mixed together, and have each child scoop out a tablespoon or two for each bag

3. Cut 6-inch squares of plastic wrap (sometimes you can get different colors) and strips of curling gift ribbon to tie the jelly bean pouches. You'll need one square of plastic wrap and one ribbon per prayer card. Or, to make things easier, put the jelly beans in zip-lock bags.

COOKING CLASS

1. Each child should take one of each color jelly beans, wrap these up in a square of plastic wrap, and tie a bow around it using the ribbon.

2. The children can now tape the pouch to the front of a prayer card.

3. The children should make as many jelly bean prayer packages as time and jelly beans allow—the more you have, the more you have to share with others.

Per jelly been pouch: 32 calories, O protein, 8 g carbohydrate, O fat, O fiber, 2 mg sodium. Calories from fat: O.

A JELLY BEAN EASTER PRAYER

In my palm I hold these beans
Of different colors, all I've seen
For anything wondrous
Is sent from above
They make me think of Jesus
And this prayer about God's love
Red is for the blood he gave
Green is for the earth he made
Yellow is for the sun, the warmth it brings
Blue is for the rain, cleansing us each Spring
Black is for the sin we made
White is for the life he gave
Purple is for his pain and tears
Pink is for these brighter years

...AND GOD CREATED THE HEAVENS AND THE EARTH

The very first words in the Old Testament of the Bible are "In the beginning God created the heavens and the earth." We all live here on earth and often take it for granted. We forget that it wasn't always here. We forget that it was God who created this earth that we call home.

GENESIS 1:1-5

In the beginning God created the heavens and the earth. Now the earth was formless and empty, darkness was over the surface of the deep, and the Spirit of God was hovering over the waters.

And God said, "Let there be light," and there was light. God saw that the light was good, and he separated the light from the darkness. God called the light "day," and the darkness he called "night." And there was evening, and there was morning—the first day.

— — — —

EDIBLE EARTH BALLS

EQUIPMENT

2 large bowls
plastic wrap (optional)
measuring cups

2 large nonstick saucepans
wooden spoons

INGREDIENTS

4 tablespoons butter or margarine
8 cups miniature marshmallows
6 cups Rice Krispies cereal
6 cups Cheerios cereal

blue food coloring
green food coloring
nonstick cooking spray

TEACHER PREP

1. If the children won't have time to eat their earth balls during class, precut plastic wrap into 16 12-inch squares.

2. Measure 3 cups of Rice Krispies and 3 cups of Cheerios into each bowl (so each bowl has a total of 6 cups of cereal).

3. Add 2 tablespoons butter or margarine to each saucepan. Melt the butter over low heat. Spray the sides of each pan with cooking spray. Add 4 cups marshmallows to each pan, and stir until completely melted. Immediately remove from heat.

COOKING CLASS

1. Divide your group into two. One group can add some green food coloring to the marshmallow mixture in one of the saucepans and the other group can add some blue food coloring to the other saucepan. Stir to blend well.

2. Now pour the cereal mixture from one bowl into one of the saucepans; repeat with the remaining cereal mixture and the remaining marshmallow mixture. Stir to coat cereal well.

3. Now each child can piece their earth together using some chunks of green (that's the land) and chunks of blue (that's the water); press the pieces together into a 3-inch ball. These can be wrapped in plastic wrap and saved for later, if desired.

Makes about 16 earth balls.
Per earth ball: 173 calories, 2.4 g protein, 34 g carbohydrate, 3.5 g fat, 1 g fiber, 8 mg cholesterol, 209 mg sodium. Calories from fat: 18 percent.

ON THE SEVENTH DAY GOD RESTED

It is important to work hard and do your chores. But God made the seventh day, the Sabbath, holy. On this day he told us to rest and worship him. He felt this was so important that he made it one of the Ten Commandments. The seventh day is also a great time to be with and enjoy your family and loved ones. Does your family have a special time each week that they spend together?

GENESIS 2:1-3
Thus the heavens and the earth were completed in all their vast array.

By the seventh day God had finished the work he had been doing; so on the seventh day he rested from all his work. And God blessed the seventh day and made it holy, because on it he rested from all the work of creating that he had done.

EXODUS 20:8-10
Remember the Sabbath day by keeping it holy. Six days you shall labor and do all your work, but the seventh day is a Sabbath to the Lord your God.

PARTY SNACK MIX

EQUIPMENT

measuring spoons
2 cup glass measure or small,
 microwave-safe mixing bowl

large, microwave-safe mixing bowl
measuring cups
paper cups

INGREDIENTS

2 tablespoons butter or margarine
1 teaspoon seasoning salt (or 1/4 teaspoon garlic powder, 1/4 teaspoon
 onion powder, and 1/4 teaspoon salt)
2 tablespoons honey

1 1/2 tablespoons Worcestershire sauce
8 cups of your favorite Chex cereals
 (corn, rice, wheat, and/or bran)
1 1/2 cups less-salt pretzel sticks
1/2 cup lightly salted mixed nuts,
 cashews, or peanuts

TEACHER PREP

1. Get equipment and ingredients ready.

COOKING CLASS

1. Children can help you measure and add the butter, seasoning salt, honey, and Worcestershire sauce to 2 cup glass measure or microwave-safe bowl. Microwave on high for a minute or two to melt butter; stir mixture.

2. Meanwhile, children can measure and mix the cereal, pretzels, and nuts in the large bowl.

3. Drizzle the butter mixture over the cereal mixture and stir to evenly coat.

4. Microwave on high for 2 minutes. Have a child toss mixture well. Microwave another 2 minutes and toss mixture. Microwave another minute or so if needed for desired crispness.

5. The children can scoop paper cups into the mixture to make individual servings that can be passed out.

Makes 18 1/2-cup servings.
Per serving: 105 calories, 2 g protein, 16.5 g carbohydrate, 3.4 g fat, 1.3 g fiber, 0 cholesterol, 200 mg sodium. Calories from fat: 29 percent.

INDEX OF LESSONS
AND RECIPES

INDEX OF BIBLE VERSES